FLYING HIGH

FLYING HIGH

Written and Photographed by
Bill Powers

Reading Consultants
Irene Swinburne
Laurence Swinburne

A TARGET BOOK

R.L. 2.9 Spache Modified Formula
EDL Core Vocabulary
For Library of Congress Cataloging in Publication Data, see page 48
Copyright © 1978 by William Powers
All rights reserved
Printed in the United States of America
5   4   3   2   1

FRANKLIN WATTS
New York / London / 1978

Karen rubbed her feet in the **rosin** and stood beside the **beam.** The gym grew still. The judge nodded and Karen mounted the beam.

Lillian, her friend and teammate, held her breath every time Karen worked the beam. She was the gutsiest girl on the team, but she was also reckless. Her beam routine was a high-wire act. When the fans watched Karen, they sat on the edge of their seats, waiting for disaster. The rest of the team called her "Evel Knievel." During practice, the boys on the basketball team would stop and watch her in amazement.

Loosening-up
exercises can help
prevent injury.

Rosin—A substance that is rubbed on gymnasts' slippers to prevent slipping.
Beam (balance beam)—A 16-foot 3-inch wooden beam mounted 4 feet off the floor.
   The top is 4 inches wide.

5

Lillian looked over at Carol Rennick, their coach. She turned to Lillian and shook her head.

Karen dismounted and the home crowd cheered.

Next up was Belinda Brown from Tranton High. The crowd was hushed. Belinda began her routine. Her control was flawless. Her **combinations** were as smooth as silk. Karen sat with her chin in her hands, staring at her. Belinda ended with a beautiful **aerial walkover dismount.** The crowd burst into applause.

Concentration is important on the 4-inch-wide beam.

Combinations—A series of moves that make up a routine.
Aerial walkover dismount—Facing the end of the beam, the gymnast throws herself in the air. With her legs in a split, she does a somersault and lands on her feet.

Karen's score went up. It was 7.75. Her teammates cheered. They watched the messenger pick up the judges' scores for Belinda's routine. The crowd waited in anticipation.

Belinda's score went up. It was 7.80. The boos and cheers rose in the air. Karen walked over to Belinda and congratulated her. Then she ran back to the bench, kicked her warm-up jacket against the wall, and sat down.

Coach Rennick sat down beside her. "Karen, you rushed again. You lost too many points on form. You've got one week before the individuals, and you've got to work hard. You'll beat Belinda when you stop beating yourself. You understand?"

Karen nodded.

"Okay," said the coach. "See you Monday."

A gymnast has to keep moving.

9

THE WORKOUTS

The gym sounded like a small, busy factory. There was the squeak made by rosin-rubbed feet spinning on the beam, and the slap of feet as they hit the mats. The **uneven bars** rattled as girls slammed their hips against them. The **springboards** bounced as they vaulted across the horse.

Karen was sitting cross-legged on the beam, arguing with Coach Rennick.

"Karen, second place isn't so bad. You deserve a medal."

"I want first place. I've got to beat Belinda, and I can with the **walkovers** and the **layout dismount.**"

"You don't have the time. You won't place at all."

"I've got to take the chance. I can't play it safe. It's my last shot at her."

Gymnasts use chalk to keep their hands dry.

Uneven bars (uneven parallel bars)—A pair of steel bars mounted on stands. The forward one, the low bar, is 4 feet 11 inches above the ground. The high bar is 7 feet 6½ inches off the ground.

Springboard—A small takeoff platform used for vaulting and mounts onto the uneven bars and beam.

Walkover—The gymnast puts her hands on the beam and kicks her legs one at a time over her head. Then one foot at a time lands on the beam. This move is also used on the floor.

Layout dismount—A back somersault where the legs are straight and the body arched.

11

Karen looked at her coach. She was wearing her stubborn, determined look. Mrs. Rennick knew it well. She often wished her other athletes had that same fire in them.

"You win," said the coach. "Get the tape."

Karen measured off the length of the beam on the red out-of-bounds line of the basketball court. She put two strips of adhesive tape to mark off the distance, 16 feet 3 inches.

"Now, don't forget the rest of your routine. It needs work."

"I won't," said Karen.

Coach Rennick rolled up the measuring tape.

"Karen, it's a tough dismount."

"Mrs. Rennick, I've got to try."

"I think you're crazy, but all right. Do the walkovers first. You've done them on the floor before. Now you've got to work on accuracy. Your hands and feet must land right on the red line or it's no good. And just short of the tape so you'll be in position for your dismount. It must be perfect. Right on the line."

All moves should first be practiced on the floor.

13

Karen began the grueling task. Over and over. Over and over. Getting one right, missing the next. For two days she kept it up, stopping only when her arms and back ached so much she had to quit.

On Wednesday, she was hitting it every time. She began to work on the rest of her routine. Her other combinations had to place her at the right spot on the beam for her walkovers and dismount.

Coach Rennick stood on the basketball court, watching her.

"Don't pause between moves. Keep it flowing. Point your toes. And get your arms higher on those turns. Otherwise they'll deduct points. . . . Okay, take a break."

Form is important in all moves.

15

Five minutes later, Karen hopped up on the beam and paced off the distance from the end of the beam to where she would begin her walkovers. Lillian and another girl were **spotting** for her. She looked down at them.

"Here goes nothing." And she did the double walkover and landed perfectly, right on the end of the beam.

"Not bad," said Lillian. "Not bad. Okay, let's try again."

But that was it for the afternoon. Karen couldn't repeat it. She started to push. But she kept slipping and falling. Lillian and the other girl saved her from getting hurt badly, but she wouldn't stop.

Gymnasts help each other when working on new moves.

Spotting—Giving a helping hand if a gymnast needs it to complete a move.

"Karen, that's enough," Lillian said. "Look at yourself."

Her legs were bruised, and both elbows were skinned. But she hopped up on the beam again.

"Karen, don't—you're gonna get hurt."

"I'll get it. I know I will." Her face was red and wet with sweat.

"*Karen!*" It was Coach Rennick. "That's enough. You're too tired. You'll kill yourself."

Karen came down off the beam and fell on her back. She was exhausted.

Coach Rennick squatted down beside her. "Karen, go home. Now. And get some rest."

In moves along the beam, the back should be straight.

19

On Friday, Karen's guts and daring paid off. The dismount seemed to come naturally. Flying was easy. She was landing on her feet every time. But her form needed work.

"Karen, keep your head back. Hands by your sides. And your legs, they've got to be straight. Do it again."

All day Saturday, Karen worked on fixing up the entire routine. It became smoother and smoother. Her **dismount** now had the height and grace of a springboard dive into water. She felt good.

When she was too tired to work anymore, Karen sat down and watched Lillian go over her floor routine. She was brooding about the championship.

One try, that's all you get. In competition, that's all you get. They don't care how hard you worked, or how many times you got it right in practice. One try and it better be good.

In a back dismount the gymnast has to "look" for the floor.

Dismount—Getting off the uneven bars or the balance beam. The final movement of a routine.

THE CHAMPIONSHIP MEDALS

There were more than a hundred gymnasts on the gym floor. The huge crowd was pressed up against the barriers, trying to get a close look at the athletes.

The girls lined up and took turns warming up. Lillian looked around for Karen. She saw her sitting by herself in the bleachers.

Team spirit helps mold good gymnasts.

23

Finally an official voice boomed from the loudspeaker.

"All spectators, please leave the floor and take your seats. **Floor** and **vaulting** will be first. Beam and uneven bars after intermission."

Karen sat in the stands with the rest of the team while the girls in vaulting and floor took their last-minute warm-ups.

With her eyes closed, she tried to picture herself as she did the combinations of her routine. She wanted the images to come to her in like a slow motion dream. Maybe it would keep her from rushing.

Far across the room, the vaulting had begun. The springboard rattled and bounced as the girls left the floor and vaulted across the horse.

Floor (floor exercise)—Tumbling and dance movements are performed on the floor and accompanied by music.

Vaulting—After a running start, the gymnast takes off from a springboard and dives over the horse.

Hips must be high while vaulting.

Lillian was up next on the floor. She stood still. With a slight nod she signaled Coach Rennick to start the tape recorder. Her music filled the gym.

Karen sat on the sideline and watched her friend. Lillian looked like a happy child. As she moved through her routine, the music seemed to lift her off the ground. When she tumbled, her body arched high over the mat. She was suspended. Her **cartwheels** and dance movements were as fine as a ballerina's.

Why do I fight so much? thought Karen. Why don't I enjoy it the way she does?

As the music built to a crescendo, Lillian finished her routine with two back **handsprings** and a high layout back **somersault.** She landed clean as a dart just as the music ended. The crowd cheered. Karen jumped up and gave a yell. Coach Rennick lifted Lillian into the air.

Floor routines look like dancing.

Cartwheel—A tumbling movement. The gymnast puts her hands on the floor and uses her arms and legs like the spokes of a wheel.
Handspring—The gymnast dives forward, lands on her hands, throws her legs over her head, and lands on her feet.
Somersault—A tumble in the air.

27

The warm-ups for the uneven bars and beam began after intermission. Karen lined up with the other girls. Just in front of her was Belinda Brown, the girl she would have to beat. She watched Belinda warm up. Belinda was as smooth as usual. She ran slowly through her routine and dismounted. Karen began to tense up. She mounted and did some stretches and spins and her side handstand. When she dismounted and ran back to the stands, the butterflies started to come.

The warm-up ended, and a meet official read the lineups for the bars and beam. Karen was first on beam. First up on the uneven bars was Julie Sheed, one of the best gymnasts in the city. The fans loved her.

The gymnasts arrive early for their warm-ups.

29

There was not a sound in the gym as the girls waited for the judges' signals. Karen let Julie begin her routine before she mounted. The uneven bars shook as Julie went through her quick, twisting combinations. Karen mounted the beam and began her routine. But she seemed angry, as if she were trying to hurt the beam. To beat it up.

Lillian's heart jumped to her throat. "Oh, no," she moaned. "Karen, slow down."

Karen's moves were sure, but they were too fast. She was headed for disaster.

Lillian saw Coach Rennick get up and cross the gym. She stopped near the far wall in line with the end of the beam. As if somehow Karen would sense her presence. But Karen seemed lost in a speeded-up dream. It was all wrong.

Quick hands are important on the uneven bars.

31

Julie was winding up her routine. She took a last swing and started her dismount. At that moment, Karen began a side handstand, her back to the audience.

Another wave of shock hit Lillian. "What if they applaud?"

Julie sprang over the high bar in a soaring dismount and made a perfect landing as the applause broke out.

It was like an explosion. Karen's hand slipped. She hit the beam with her shoulder and fell hard onto the mat.

Lillian whispered, "Oh, no."

Karen got up, finished her routine, and ran from the gym.

The judges watch the competitors closely.

33

Lillian and the other girls ran after her as Coach Rennick headed for the officials' table.

They found Karen in the small practice gym. She was crying. Lillian put her arm around her. She had never seen Karen cry before.

"I was awful," Karen sobbed. "Awful. I did it again."

Then over the public address system they heard, "Because of the applause, the contestant from Barron High will have the opportunity to repeat her routine at the end of the regular competition."

The girls cheered and pounded Karen on the back. She didn't even look up.

Feelings run high in close competition.

35

Mrs. Rennick came in. "Girls, go back to the gym. I'll be out in a minute."

Lillian was watching Belinda. Her routine was beautiful. She scored an 8.5 and easily led the other competitors. Lillian thought, Karen doesn't have a chance.

In the practice gym, Coach Rennick sat beside Karen.

"Mrs. Rennick, how could I? I did it again."

"Karen, listen to me. Don't say anything. Just listen. I can't say for sure how the judges would have scored you if you hadn't fallen. But the applause was a break for you. Karen, you're getting what none of the other girls out there is getting. Not one of them. You're getting a second chance."

Mrs. Rennick stood up.

Karen lifted her head. She began to wipe away the tears.

Coach Rennick started back to the main gym. Karen bent over and gingerly touched her ankle. It had begun to swell.

Arms should look graceful and strong.

Coach Rennick came over to Lillian. "Get Karen. She'll be on in five minutes." Lillian got up and ran into the practice gym.

"Karen, Mrs. Rennick sent me to . . ."

Karen interrupted her. "Get me some tape."

"What? You're up next."

"Some tape. My ankle."

"Are you hurt?"

"Just hurry. *Please*—and don't say anything."

Lillian ran to the locker room and brought back a roll of adhesive tape.

"Wrap it," said Karen. "Tight as you can."

Karen winced as Lillian wrapped her ankle.

Gymnasts feel awful after a bad routine.

39

There was applause in the main gym. Karen got up and headed for the doors just as her name was announced. Lillian followed her. She knew Karen was in pain. But Karen trotted over to the rosin box, rubbed her feet in the powder, and took up her position beside the beam.

She stood quietly and waited for the judges' nod.

Lillian ran over to Coach Rennick.

"Her ankle. She hurt her ankle."

"The poor kid," said the coach. "She tries so hard."

The judges deduct points for any false moves.

41

Lillian didn't want to look, but as soon as Karen mounted the beam she saw this time it would be different. From the moment Karen touched the beam, the excitement of her routine came alive. It was clear and clean. And time seemed to slow down as Karen moved through the most beautiful routine Lillian had ever seen.

All beam moves should flow smoothly.

43

Coach Rennick began to smile as she waited for Karen's dismount. When the moment came, it was high and neat and perfect.

The fans jumped to their feet and applauded. They didn't have to wait for the judges' score. They knew who had taken first place.

As Karen limped off the floor, Lillian and Coach Rennick and the rest of the girls ran down to meet her.

Karen put her arm around Lillian's shoulders to take the weight off her sore ankle. Coach Rennick took hold of Karen's other arm and squeezed her. "You're crazy," she said. And Karen's face broke into a broad grin.

Victory is the payoff for long months of hard work.

45

GLOSSARY

Rosin—A substance that is rubbed on gymnasts' slippers to prevent slipping.

Beam (balance beam)—A 16-foot 3-inch wooden beam mounted 4 feet off the floor. The top is 4 inches wide.

Combinations—A series of moves that make up a routine.

Aerial walkover dismount—Facing the end of the beam, the gymnast throws herself in the air. With her legs in a split, she does a somersault and lands on her feet.

Uneven bars (uneven parallel bars)—A pair of steel bars mounted on stands. The forward one, the low bar, is 4 feet 11 inches above the ground. The high bar is 7 feet 6½ inches off the ground.

Springboard—A small takeoff platform used for vaulting and mounts onto the uneven bars and beam.

Walkover—The gymnast puts her hands on the beam and kicks her legs one at a time over her head. Then one foot at a time lands on the beam. This move is also used on the floor.

Spotting—Giving a helping hand if a gymnast needs it to complete a move.

Layout dismount—A back somersault where the legs are straight and the body arched.

Dismount—Getting off the uneven bars or the balance beam. The final movement of a routine.

Floor (floor exercise)—Tumbling and dance movements are performed on the floor and accompanied by music.

Vaulting—After a running start, the gymnast takes off from a springboard and dives over the horse.

Cartwheel—A tumbling movement. The gymnast puts her hands on the floor and uses her arms and legs like the spokes of a wheel.

Handspring—The gymnast dives forward, lands on her hands, throws her legs over her head, and lands on her feet.

Somersault—A tumble in the air.

ABOUT THE AUTHOR
AND PHOTOGRAPHER

Bill Powers' special talents include photography and the theater. As director-founder of the Second Story Players in New York City, he won the coveted Obie Award for the high quality of his productions. Now Mr. Powers has brought his fine sense of drama and visual expression to *Flying High*.
Mr. Powers is also the author of *Break Him Down!* (A Target Book) and *The Weekend*, a high-interest, controlled-vocabulary novel in Franklin Watts' new Triumph series.

Library of Congress Cataloging in Publication Data

Powers, Bill.
  Flying high.

  (A Target book)
  SUMMARY: Karen wants desperately to win the gymnastics championship but she is her own "worst enemy."
  [1. Gymnastics—Fiction] I. Title.
PZ7.P8834Fl   [Fic]   77-14290
ISBN 0-531-01461-4